Devoran
& its River

a photographic history

To Sid & Jane
With best wishes
Ralph
& Marie

Ralph & Marie Bird

24/10/2008

truran

Acknowledgements

This 'Devoran and its River - *a photographic history*' is the result of many years' work and collecting photographs. However, as the book progressed, many people kindly allowed us to use photographs from their own collections. Without these additional pictures, this book would have been that much poorer.

The pictures vary in quality, as they were taken with an ordinary camera, however, each picture is an event in Devoran's history, so better a poor photograph than none at all.

We are indebted to the following people for their help. They are, in alphabetical order: Bob Acton, Graham Crocker, Aubrey Ferris, Peter George, Jean Lapham, Bill Marshall, the late Betty Phillips, Jill Roskilly and Jo Sedgemoor.

Also to Geoff and Liz Aver, for checking the proofs and to our publishers Ivan and Heather Corbett for their help and support.

We hope that after reading this book, people will come forward with other photographs and - who knows - maybe it will lead to Volume 2.

Ralph and Marie Bird
Carnon Mine 2008.

Published 2008 by Truran, Croft Prince, Mount Hawke, Truro, Cornwall TR4 8EE.
www.truranbooks.co.uk
Truran is an imprint of Truran Books Ltd
ISBN 978 185022 224 8

Typeset by Marie Bird of Devoran
4 Carnon Mine, Devoran, Truro, Cornwall. TR3 6NG.

Printed and bound in Great Britain by R Booth Ltd
The Praze, Penryn, Cornwall. TR10 8AA.

In Memory of David Rowe

Introduction

Devoran once played a major part in Cornwall's industrial heritage. The deepwater channel, which brought schooners, barges and steam coasters up to the village, has long silted up. Now, only small leisure craft use the river.

The days of Devoran as a port ended in 1915, when the Redruth and Chacewater Railway closed. The railway took coal up to the mines around St. Day and Redruth and brought back copper and tin ore for smelting. When the railway ended, so did Devoran as a port - one depended on the other.

The photographs in this book show not only Devoran as a port with its railway, but also aspects of village life as it used to be.

There were two shipyards on the river - one at the end of Devoran Quay, the other at Carnon Yard.

Two hundred years ago alluvial tin streaming was another major industry on the river.

Devoran has indeed played its part in Cornwall's industrial past. Today, it is just a quiet backwater, its river used only for leisure.

Devoran and its River

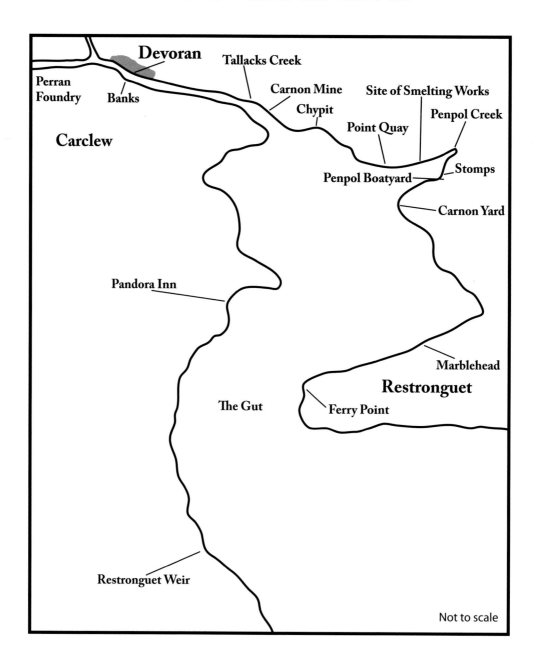

Perran Foundry

Devoran

Banks

Carclew

Tallacks Creek

Carnon Mine

Chypit

Site of Smelting Works

Point Quay

Penpol Creek

Penpol Boatyard

Stomps

Carnon Yard

Pandora Inn

Marblehead

Restronguet

The Gut

Ferry Point

Restronguet Weir

Not to scale

Perran Foundry c. 1900.

Perran Foundry, after it had ceased to be a foundry. Started in 1791, it was built by the Fox family of Falmouth, later taken over by Williams. It was famous for its engineering and castings. In the 1840s the main beam at Tresavean Mine broke. Fox's Foundry - as it was then - cast a new beam and delivered it in four days. The beam weighed 26 tons. The foundry later became Edwards' Flour Mill, but now lies empty.

Double Quays in the Perran Channel c. 1910.

The barge is discharging her cargo into the lighter. This is apparent as there is a gin block rigged on the end of the gaff. The cargo is probably grain to be taken to Edwards' Mill just up the river.

Houseboat in the Perran Channel.

The vessel in the picture is an old barge named 'Queen'. She was built by Scoble and Davies at Malpas in the 1880s. During the 1930s she was converted into a houseboat by Frank Peters of St. Mawes. She won the cup for the most miles cruised in one year from the Royal Cruising Club sailing down to France and through the French canals.

Right after the war, she was moved to the Perran channel and used as a holiday home.
In the early 1960s she parted her moorings and drifted across a mud bank and broke her back. Shortly after she was broken up.

Carnon Valley.

This is the Carnon Valley between Bissoe and Devoran, showing one of Brunel's viaducts, built of timber and granite. There were many of these structures in the county when the Great Western Railway was built in the 1840s.

Carnon Valley Viaduct.

The old wooden viaducts were replaced later by ones built entirely of granite and brick: this shows the second Bissoe viaduct under construction.

The Main Truro to Falmouth Road.

These two girls are happily posing for this picture taken just above the main Truro - Falmouth road. The house on the extreme right is Poplar Cottage.

Two Boys Swimming in the River.

These two boys are swimming in the Devoran river, near what is now Devoran Joinery.

The stack was once part of Devoran Brickworks.

Redruth and Chacewater Railway Weighbridge.
This is the weighbridge for the Redruth and Chacewater Railway just off the main road. It must have been taken after 1915, when the railway closed, as there is no sign of any track either side of the weighbridge.

Devoran Local Band.
This band was formed by Jonathon Webber, a carpenter employed by the Redruth and Chacewater Railway Company, in their workshops at Devoran. The band consisted of his sons and a nephew and were known locally as the 'Billy Cock Hat Band'. The band entered contests at Truro and was engaged in playing at Tea Treats in the district and at social events held at *Bosahan* on the Helford River. They practised on the lawn at Weighbridge House - the home of the Webber family for 105 years. This photograph was taken some time before 1894. The drummer is Jonathon's son, Edward.

The Old Toll House on the Main Road.

It was demolished in the early 1960s for road widening, which actually did not happen.

Devoran in the 1960s.

This picture was taken in the early 1960s and may appear to have changed little. It is taken by the pond, which is called Woodbury Pond, on the western side of the main Truro to Falmouth road, but long before the housing developments at Tremayne Close and Edwards' Road, in the fields just left of centre at the top. The gate keeper's cottage just to the right of row of cottages on the left-hand side of the picture was demolished in the 1980s.

Devoran from Banks c. 1910.

Devoran from Banks c. 2000.

A modern photograph of the village - it shows new housing along the river bank with little evidence that Devoran was once a busy industrial port.

Devoran from Banks c. 1920.

The docks closed in 1915 so there are no ships to be seen. The banks were, and to a lesser extent still are, a favourite place for family picnics.

Carclew Deer Park, with Deer in the Field.

Devoran as a port has died - there are no ships alongside the quays, so the picture was probably taken after 1915.

Devoran from Carclew.

A well known scene of Devoran, taken in 1900 from Carclew Estate, clearly shows the terraces, church, chapel and school. The upper quays are all intact, but there are no vessels in sight. Devoran as a port had passed its peak and trading vessels were getting fewer.

Devoran from Carclew.

The same scene a hundred years later - 2000 - and the changes can clearly be seen. The village itself has changed little apart from the quays and docks which have long gone and now houses and bungalows stretch along the water's edge. Now only small craft can reach Devoran and then only on a big tide.

Devoran Docks c. 1900.

Not as active as previous years. By 1900, the warning signs were there and this picture shows just two schooners alongside the quays.

Devoran Quay c. 1910.

It is difficult to imagine Devoran a hundred years ago as a busy port compared with the quiet backwater it has become in modern times. The steamer is Monk's 'Greta'.

Devoran Quay 1910.

This photograph is well known and has been used many times in other publications but often printed the wrong way round. She is a Welsh schooner called the 'C. S. Spooner'. There is another schooner lying astern.

Devoran Quay 1912.
This group of boys have been allowed to play in the schooner's boat. The bow of the schooner can just be seen in the background. Left to right: —?; —?; Bernard Hitchens (Joe); Melville Hitchens; —?; —?; Thomas Hart Hitchens; — Tregaskis. Note the wooden fenders fixed to the side of the boat.

PERRAN R, FROM DEVORAN.

Devoran Quay 1905.
This is a rare picture of the upper Quay - another example of Devoran as a port.
The 'Erimus' is shown moored above what is now Devoran Boatyard. It would be almost impossible now for anything much bigger than a rowing boat to reach this part of the river. The picture was taken from Devoran playing field. The steamer has probably discharged her cargo of steam coal from South Wales as she is floating light. Before sailing she will probably load a cargo of copper ore to take back.

Devoran Quay c. 1912.
The 'Erimus' - one of several vessels that came to Devoran.

The 'Mary' of Truro.

The 'Mary' of Truro - not to be confused with the 'Mary' of Plymouth. She was built at the end of Narabo Quay by Hugh Eddy Stephens in 1875. She was actually designed by Charles George, who worked for him. She weighed 50 tons and was run for most of her working life by the Trebilcock family who at that time lived at Bleak House, Carnon Mine. She was sold in 1946 to Appledore owners for carrying gravel. In 1958 she ended up on the Sharpness and Gloucester canal, where she was abandoned. This picture shows her approaching Devoran Quay on a quiet day, as she is sailing with all her sails up.

'Mary' of Plymouth c. 1910.

This barge is shown discharging her cargo in Vivian's Dock. The barge is below quay level. At the present time the maximum depth is about three feet. This barge is often mistaken for the 'Mary' of Truro, but they were two different vessels. If proof were needed, the bowsprit of the 'Mary' of Truro came out on the starboard side of her stemhead, whereas on the Plymouth 'Mary' it came out on the port side. Also the cuddy or cabin, where men lived if they stayed aboard, was forward on the Plymouth 'Mary' (the smoke stack can be seen in front of the mast), but on the 'Mary' of Truro her cuddy was aft, as in her photograph, the smoke stack can be seen almost back by the tiller. Also anyone with an eye for ships can see this barge hasn't the beautiful lines of the Truro 'Mary'.

S. S. 'Trefusis' leaving Fowey c. 1910.

Although this picture is taken at Fowey, the S.S. 'Trefusis' was one of the vessels that regularly used the port of Devoran. She is probably carrying a cargo of china clay.

Devoran Docks from the Banks c. 1910.

Looking at the river today, it is difficult to believe that ships of this size came so far up the river to Devoran. The ships are (left to right) 'Treleigh', 'Plover' and 'Erimus'. This picture shows, perhaps more than any other, what Devoran used to be like as a port. Will Trebilcock once told me that on a spring tide there used to be sixteen feet of water off the end of Devoran Quay.

Devoran Regatta 1910.

Local regattas were a major event in the social calendar. The quays either side of Vivian's Dock are crowded with spectators who have come to watch the rowing and sailing matches. One of the local pleasure steamers has also made its way up the river.

Devoran Docks c. 1906.

This is the 'Roseland', one of many pleasure steamers on the River Fal. On the back of the original postcard is written: "This steamer will leave Devoran on Saturday 15th July at 6.15 p.m. prompt." It is postmarked 1907. Further down the quay are two schooners.

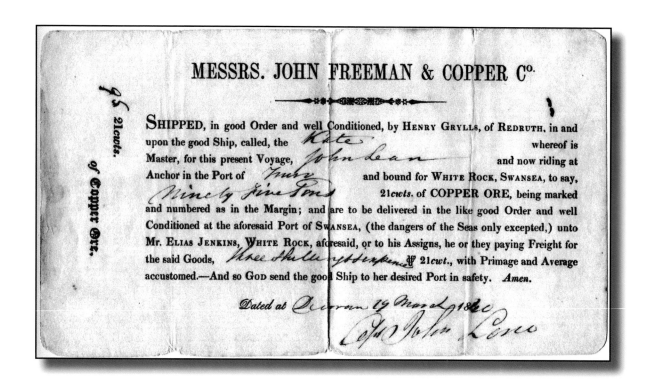

One of the Cargo Tariffs for Copper Ore.

Group: St. John's Terrace, behind the pub, 'The Commercial' c. 1914.

These are men from a sailing ship in Devoran Docks. There are also local men in the picture, although the only one that can be named is Jim Ferris, or Jim Tack as he was known, on the left of the picture. The picture was taken at the rear of the pub we now know as the 'Old Quay Inn'. There were a number of pubs to choose from in the village around this time: the 'Robartes' and the 'Crown & Anchor' were just two of them.

Lower Quay after being Bought by the Village in the 1980s.

In the 1980s, after much fund-raising by locals and successful application for grants, Devoran bought the quay and dock. Much work was carried out by volunteers and the photographs show the rebuilding of the quays. This was done in various stages, over a period of time as funds allowed.

Lower Quay Repairs.

Hugh Rowe's Coal Store in Quay Road c. 1948.

Railway workmen outside building which is now the Village Hall.

This is a scene taken in the early 1900s and shows some of the men who worked on the railway. From left to right they are: Richard Burrows - blacksmith; Jonathon Webber - carpenter; William Andrewartha - engineer; Tom Tregaskis - carpenter; Walter Webber - line man; Tom Tregaskis - fitter. It is just coincidence that the name Tom Tregaskis appears twice and is not a mistake. Each man is holding the tool appropriate to his trade. The picture is behind what is now Devoran Village Hall, but was then the engine workshop. William Andrewartha was later killed in a bicycle accident near Treluswell.

'Spitfire', one of the Three Redruth and Chacewater Railway Engines.

Railway Workers c. 1910.
Two railway employees with one of the ponies used on the railway.

'Miner', another of the Redruth and Chacewater Railway Engines.

Railway Workers c. 1910.

These are some of the men employed by the Redruth and Chacewater Railway. The names are not known but each man is holding the tool of his trade.

Railway Engine 'Miner' c. 1910.
The man on the left is Tommy Lavin. The picture was taken on Quay Road, just below Olive Villas.

'Smelter'.
Another of the engines that made up the Devoran to Chacewater Railway. Many people find it difficult to believe that a railway ran through Devoran.

Engine in Carclew Terrace.

The engine is situated in what is now the village hall car park. The cottage on the right was the 'Robartes Arms', one of several public houses in the village.

Carclew View, Devoran

Carclew Terrace c. 1950/60s.

Showing the village hall before the extension. The main entrance opens directly into the car park. Just one vehicle, the local greengrocer Frank Collins' van, in the car park.

Redruth and Chasewater Rly   Devoran Quay

An Early Picture of the Railway in Devoran c. 1900. The engine is just outside the workshop, now Quay House. The white posts show the path leading to Tank Hill.

Devoran Quay c. 1915.

This group of men are dismantling the railway track. In front of them are lines and chairs. With the ending of the railway, the docks were doomed - one supported the other. The men are all local and include: Charlie Marshall; Eddie Marshall; William Curnow; Charlie Culliver; Tom Wilcox; Ned Tregaskis; Josiah Marshall; Billy Quick; Jim Wilcox; — Rowe; Fred Mitchell.

Occupation Classification No.	Code No. of Office of Issue	Volunteer's Enrolment No.
182	*1909*	*65*

EMPLOYMENT EXCHANGE,

Redruth

2nd Aug 191*8*.

SIR,

WAR WORK VOLUNTEER.

I have to inform you that, in accordance with the terms of your enrolment as a War Work Volunteer, you are hereby directed to present yourself for work

on *6th August 1918*

at *The Parkgate Iron & Steel Co Ltd*

Rotherham

*A Railway Warrant for the journey is enclosed.
  * Strike out if unnecessary.

A form of claim is also enclosed. This form is for use only if you desire to claim, in accordance with the terms of your enrolment, any of the following :—

(a) a daily subsistence allowance; or
(b) a daily travelling allowance; or
(c) a daily travelling allowance and one hour's travelling time per day at the rate of time and a half; or
(d) any difference in rate of wages.

The claim (if any) should be dealt with by you in the manner shewn on the form of claim.

It is essential that you should commence work on the date specified.

In the event of any misunderstanding arising as to payment or conditions, the facts will be considered by the Minister after your work has been begun. You should not on this account defer starting work or leave your work. Any complaint should be made at once to the Manager of the local Employment Exchange, who has instructions to transmit it to the Minister of National Service.

Your new employer has been asked to notify the local Employment Exchange when he no longer requires your services, and in that event you must at once report the fact to the nearest Employment Exchange, when you will be required to fill in a Form for transmission to the Minister relating to the circumstances under which you have left your employment, and to state the Numbers on your Certificate of Enrolment. The same Numbers appear at the head of this Form.

I am,

Your obedient Servant,

R D (signature)

Manager.

To *Mr E Webber*

Carnon Gate Devoran Cornwall

[W1029]   100m   10/17   G & S

When the Devoran - Chacewater Railway closed, Ed Webber had to drive a train in the Rotherham Iron and Steelworks as a part of the war effort.

Picnic over Banks c. 1910.

This was a favourite summer pastime for people. Unfortunately the names of these people have not survived, except for the man in the middle of the picture, who was named Andrewartha.

St. John's Terrace c. 1900.

It would be wonderful to know who the old gentleman is. A view like this would be almost impossible to take in this day and age, because of the number of cars on the road.

St. John's Terrace.
Only the lack of cars tells us that it was taken many years ago.

Belmont Terrace c. 1900.
This is the 'Back Terrace'; the picture was probably taken from the churchyard.

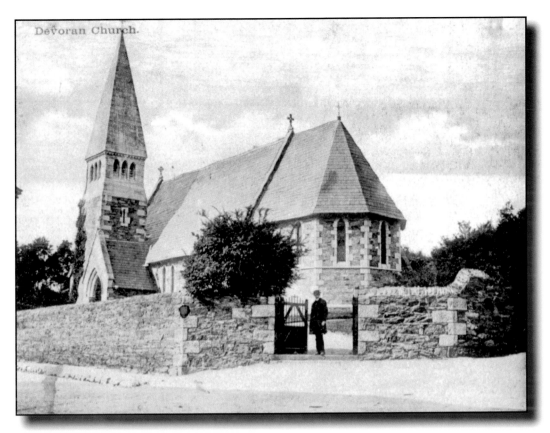

Devoran Church 29th January 1906.

Devoran Church was built in 1875, to the design of J. Pearson who also designed Truro Cathedral. Although Devoran has its own church, it is in the Parish of Feock.

Compare this modern picture of Devoran Church taken in 2004.

Devoran Football Team 1906. All unnamed.

Devoran Football Team 1920 /21.

The venue is unknown but some of the team are named. Back row: 1st - Mr. Martin; 4th - Percy Trenoweth; 7th - Rev'd John Jones; Front row: 3rd - Will Trebilcock; 4th - Bunnie Dunstan; 6th - Charlie Trebilcock; 7th - Bert Nicholls.

Looking down Market Street c. 1923.

The pavements and the gutters are still cobbled and the road still fairly rough. The trees in Carclew Wood are in leaf. It could be Autumn, as in the original picture, the poster in the top shop doorway is advertising a Harvest Festival. Halfway down the street on the right hand side, there are two further shops, opposite the Market House, which is on the left of the picture.

Taken the same time, c. 1923, but looking up Market Street.

Who are the people? The two small boys appear to have a wooden scooter to play with.

Dick Bryant with his Traps.
Like many others, he earned his living in many ways. He was a poacher, oysterman, fisherman and barge man, working for many years on the Devoran barge, 'Maggie', with the owner Joe Nicholls.

Wesleyan Group, St. John's Terrace 1913.
The Wesleyan School Group, marching along St. John's Terrace.

Church Army Caravan.
Church Army Caravans were a normal sight in the 1890s. They travelled around the country spreading the 'good word'. This is taken in Market House Square.

Devoran W. I. Choir.

The year is not certain, but probably around 1895. This is Devoran W. I. Choir. The gentleman in the front centre is Mr. Cock, the head teacher at Devoran School.

Church Sunday School Tea Treat c. 1905.

This was an annual event, held at Devoran House.

Devoran Church Tea Treat c. 1909.

Dick Trebilcock is 2nd right in the middle wearing a bowler hat. Also in the picture are William and Charles Trebilcock. Note the saffron buns - known as Tea Treat Buns - the size of a dessert plate.

Sunday School Tea Treat - 1910.

Among the children in the front row is Myrtle Kernick (neé Shepperd).

Chapel Tea Treat.

Not Devoran Church Tea Treat, but Devoran Chapel - the year is 1911. The two girls in bridesmaids' outfits are Phyllis and Gladys Webber.

Devoran Church Tea Treat, Devoran 1919.

This was an annual event each summer, but, like all village community events, it has died away.

Devoran Carnival c. 1920.

Another event in village life - this is Devoran Carnival around 1920. It appears to be a contest for the best decorated bicycle.

Devoran Chapel.

This could have been taken in modern times except that between the chapel and the cottage, on the right, there is a schooner tied up at the docks, so it had to be taken before 1915, when the docks closed. The chapel was built in 1856, several years before the church was built in Devoran.

An Early View of Market Street – July 1904.

The cobbled pavements and road can clearly be seen. Also the railway is still going strong as the level crossing gates are very apparent.

Level Crossing Gates 1904.
Almost the same scene but with a pony and trap and all the people looking at the camera.

Bottom of Market Street.

At the time of this photograph, there is little change in this view of Market Street, taken in the early 1950s. Ronnie Moore's bakery and shop is now established along with his car. At the time of writing two cottages have since replaced the bakery and shop, which was the last remaining shop in Devoran.

St. John's Terrace with one of Dungey's Coaches Parked up.

This would have been taken around the 1890s. Dungey operated these horse-drawn coaches from Devoran to Truro, Falmouth and Redruth.

House in St. John's Terrace c. 1910.
Were the lady and gentleman someone special to have their picture taken outside their house?

Market Street c. 1900.
Market Street seems to be a popular venue for photographers. This was taken around 1900. The two pony and traps have stopped to allow the two drivers to catch up on the latest gossip.

St. John's Terrace c. 1910.

The children have been asked to pose for this photograph, as with the old box camera, the subjects had to keep perfectly still for several seconds, unlike the modern day camera, where it can be done in fractions of a second. The boy on the left with the basket has obviously been told to look after his little sister.

Market Street.

This view of Market Street is taken much later - probably in the 1950s. The road and pavements have been tarmaced. A van and a push-bike have appeared. Who are the children at the bottom of the street? The Market House can clearly be seen on the left.

DEVORAN.   1045.

Top of Market Street c. 1920.
There were several shops in Devoran, at this time, including the three in this picture.

St. John's Terrace, Devoran

St. John's Terrace c. 1910 and not a car in sight!
The lady and gentleman have obviously been asked to pose for this picture, but who are they?

Dungey's Horse Drawn Carriage.

This was public transport in the late 1800s. It shows two of Dungey's horse-drawn carriages, which operated from Devoran.

Chapel Hill 1905.

This shows the end of Belmont Terrace and the start of Chapel Terrace. The chapel is on the right.

Level Crossing Gates at the Bottom of Market Street July 1905.

The gates are shown quite clearly here. The Wesleyan School Group are marching down the hill. The gate posts can still be seen in the garden alongside.

Carclew Terrace, Devoran c. 1910.

The shop window can clearly be seen in what was the last Post Office. The docks were still active at this time. The Post Office was at that time a general stores.

Devoran School.

Devoran school was built in the 1860s and this shows the original building before alterations.

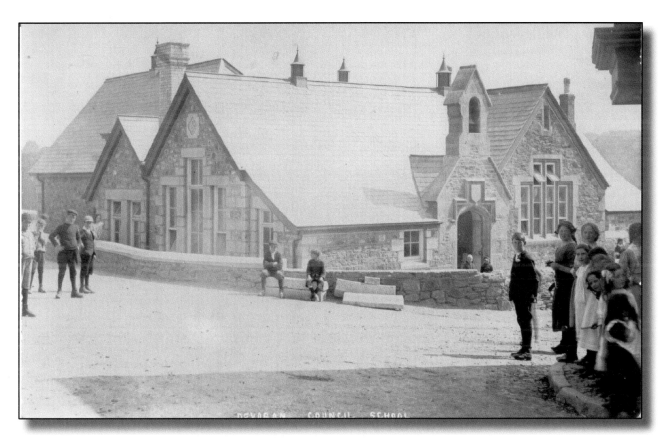

Devoran School after Alteration in the late 1870s.

The work has almost been completed, as two of he boys are sitting on the capping stones for the wall.

Class at Devoran school 1895.

All of this class are named and they include two of Ralph Bird's great aunts.

Back row (left to right): Charlie Williams; Ralph Howard Mitchell; Percy Mitchell; Tom Trebilcock; Howard Mitchell; Charlie Tonkin; Gerald Clear.

2nd row: Julia Bryant; Ethel Hodge; Beatrice Williams; Florence Johns; Bertha Hattam; May Harris; Emily Pollard; Martha Bryant.

3rd row: Maud Trebilcock; Ada Dungey; Annie Mitchell; Lily Maud Cock; Annie Nicholls; Laura Martin; Rosie Snelling; Mary Nicholls; Jane Harris.

4th Row: John Bryant; Charlie Bryant; Joe Richards; Jimmy Skewes; Walter Menear; Richard Mitchell; William Hall; Sam Williams; William Pengelly.

The Headmaster, Mr. Cock, is on the right.

There are two of my Grandfather's sisters in this photograph. Julia Bryant, who lived to be ninety-nine and Martha Bryant, who eventually went to live in New Zealand.

Teachers - Devoran School 1898.

Back (left to right): Harry Cock; — —?. Middle: Mrs. Quick; Mr. Cock; Miss Stephens.
Front: Miss Short; Ethel —?.

Teachers - Devoran School 2008.

This is the 'after' of the 'before and after' photographs. It shows the teachers in almost the same pose in June, 2008 – a hundred and ten years later. They are, starting from the back, left to right (standing): Chris Cook; Joles Varnish. Middle (sitting): Jane Foster; Lee Gardiner; Katie Thurston.
Front (kneeling) Sharon Goodreid; Becky Bowker.

This is the Official Handover of the Playing Field in 1919.
The speaker is Mr. Cock, the head teacher.

Devoran School c. 1900.
The children are actually up on the crossroads for this photograph. No fear of being knocked over by a car in those days.

Class at Devoran School c. 1900.

Back row (left to right): — —; — —; Henry Teague; Stanton Teague; Hugh Rowe; — Dungey; Robert Stephens; Humphrey White.

2nd row: Mr. Cock; Carrie Pollard; Lillian Mitchell; Dora Dungey; Lillian Pengelly; Maud Brown; Mowin Bilkey; — Rowe.

3rd row: Evelyn Mitchell; Violet Pengelly; Maggie Burrows; — Rowe; Ivy Truscott; Sarah Pollard; Elizabeth Ferris.

4th row: Jim Stephens; — —?; — — ?; Willie Richards: Mary Richards; Helen Ferris; Daisy Dungey.

Devoran School Choir c. 1905.

No-one in this picture is named. It was taken outside the church.

Devoran School c. 1920.

Left to right, back row: M Ferris; M Courage; J Courage; S Jones; S Hall; S Orchard; F Deeble; M Bryant; G Curnow; H Hawke.

2nd row: H Mansell; K Moss; A Ferris; ; P -- ?; G Burley; D Orchard; V Pellow; K Bray.

3rd row: P Williams; R King; C Bennetts; B Phillips; H Pooley; E Bray; A Johnson; N Hughes; J Burley.

4th row: J Pengelly; A Tregaskis; L Borrows; E Deeble; G Clift; J Crocker; J Lewarne; E Sullivan.

Cubs and Brownies c. 1925.

Devoran Cubs and Brownies as can be seen from their caps.

Devoran School c. 1928.

Left to right, back row: — Loosemoor; Ronnie Hawke; Victor Jenkin; — —; Wally Trenoweth; Ronnie Datson; Bill Marshall.

2nd row: Gerald Lean; — —; Inez Deeble; Winnifred Harris; — —; Marion Trebilcock; Betty Marshall; May Trembath; Tony Solomon; Ken Trenoweth.

Front row: John Lillie: Basil Tallack; — —; Reggie Clinton; Gregor Rosevear; Joe Carlyon; — —; — Loosemoor; Montague Courage; — —.

Devoran School c. 1930.

Left to right, back row: Master - Mr. Turner; Pearl Jose; Inez Deeble; May Trembath; Sylvia Thomas; Betty Marshall; Pamela Ferris; Winifred Harris.

2nd row: — —; Walter Collis; Tony Solomon; Ken Trenoweth; Lilian Jenkin; Edwina Argyle; Nancy Courage; Derby Pellow; Miles Cook; Victor Jenkin.

Front row: Donald Jeffrey; Ronnie Hawke; Gerald Lean; Wally Trenoweth; Montague Courage; Harold Hutchins; Joe Carlyon; Gregor Rosevear.

Devoran Folk Dancing Group 1920.
Another annual event in Devoran's calendar. The girl first on the left front row is Audrey Webber. The girl first left in the back row is Kitty Trebilcock. She died the following year.

DEVORAN COUNTY PRIMARY SCHOOL
CELEBRATES
VICTORY DAY
June 8th, 1946.

Presented to ....

WORLD WAR - - September 3rd, 1939
V.E. DAY Victory in Europe 8th May, 1945
V.J. DAY Victory over Japan August 15th, 1945

"THERE'LL ALWAYS BE AN ENGLAND"

= = God Save the King = =

Dad's Army.
The Home Guard for Carnon Downs and Devoran. They were all local men.

Back row: Frank Dymond; Reg Crocker; Walter Hoare; Ron Burley; Doug Connor; Lax Collins; Gerald Lean; Albert Opie; Harry Crocker.

Second Row: Jimmy Ferris; Tom Sleeman; Ken Hoare; --?; Albert Green; Ernie Pengelly; Bill Gay; Alfie Johnson; Percy Jeffrey; Stan Ford; Walter Collis; Arthur Tregaskis; Percy Nicholls; - Truan; Sid Rosevear; Jack Connor; Bill Marshall; Charlie Rosevear; --?.

Seated: Reg Mitchell; Bunny Dunstan; Harry Davey; George Knight; Harry Solomon; - Teague; Percy Hawke; - Evans; Alec Grey.

Kneeling: Alfie Williams; Henry Woolcock; Fred Knuckey; Clarence Burrows; Tom Hitchen; Gordon Clift; Charlie Bryant; Joe Carlyon; Arthur George; Bernard Pooley; - ?, Tom Barker.

A Different View of Devoran School.

This photograph of Devoran School was taken from the top of Devoran Church spire in July 1993. It shows the village playing field and the whole layout of the school including Market House. Adjacent to the playing field is the back of Carclew Terrace.

Devoran School's New Access Road being Developed.

The New Devoran School being Built 2007.

September 2007 saw the opening of Devoran's new school in Devoran Lane. It was decided to build a new school as the old one is now too small to accommodate village children and those from outlying areas.

Devoran's New School 2008.

The new school in Devoran Lane after completion. This picture was taken in June, 2008.

The 'Commercial Inn'.

Two horse drawn wagons parked outside of the 'Old Quay Inn', or, as it was known then, the 'Commercial'. What are the two discussing - maybe who was going to win what at the local regatta?

Aerial View of Devoran 1925.

This is the first known aerial photograph of Devoran, and clearly shows Belmont, Terrace, St. John's Terrace and Quay Road. Devoran was designed as a model picture village, but was never completed. There are one or two houses built at he end of Devoran Lane, but only fields where Edwards' Road, Perran Close and Tremayne Close have since been built.

Devoran Carnival 27th August 1949.

This was an annual event - now sadly ended. There are village people in the picture, including Pat Pinnick, Bill Marshall and Josephine Sedgemoor (neé George). They are seen here walking down Chapel Hill.

Devoran Carnival 27th August 1949.

The same people here, but near Devoran Bridge.

Lower Quay, Devoran, in the early 1950s showing little sign of its former glory.
Looking at this picture, it is difficult to imagine it with schooners, ketches, coasters and all the other activities that once made it one of the most important ports in the county.

Pub and Chapel 1955.
This was taken from Quay Road and shows the Chapel at the back. The 'Old Quay Inn', or the 'Commercial', as it was then known, is in the centre of the picture.

An Early Motor Car in Devoran 1930.

The girl sitting on the car bonnet is Betty King (Phillips), her mother is standing in the porch. The person on extreme left in the doorway is Minnie Dudley. The man sitting on the step is John Sanders - his wife, Annie Sanders was the post lady. Jack King is the man in the centre.

Devoran W. I.

This picture of the Devoran W. I. was taken probably in the early 1960s. Sadly, like many other of our social gatherings, it now no longer exists.

Devoran Red Cross.

Taken from behind the Village Hall, the names of the people are:

Back Row: Heather Collis; Sylvia Wilkinson; Jo Sweet; Anne Carlyon; _ ?, Megan King

Front Row: Alicia Dash; Gillian Burley; Mary Collis; Annette Ferris; Miss Audrey Webber; Sarah Montgomery; Anne White.

Dolphin at Devoran.

An unusual event for Devoran. This dolphin was stranded at Devoran Quay just before Christmas 2001. However, with the help of local people and the R.S.P.C.A. it survived and was taken to Falmouth and released.

Devoran Jubilee Celebrations 2002.
St. John's Terrace was closed to traffic and a line of tables set up. It started at the school and went all the way down to the pub. The gentleman on the left wearing shorts and dark glasses is the vicar at the time, Robert Sellers.

February 2000.
This car rolled over the wall on the right. Fortunately there was no-one in the vehicle at the time, but the car was a write-off.

Tallacks Creek.

During the summer of 2007, the road between Devoran and Point was shut for several months. This was due to the culvert under the road collapsing. The section of road across Tallacks Creek was completely dug up and re-laid.

Nonsuch.

This is a view of the cottage at Nonsuch, between Higher Devoran Farm and Tallacks Creek. Some of Ralph Bird's ancestors, Jack and Caroline Bryant and their children, were the last family to live there before it was condemned. They then moved to Carnon Mine.

Carnon Mine from Aver's Field 16th May 1905.

This is the date on the back of the original postcard. Little has changed. There is a barge coming up the river. On the left, above the hill, can be seen the stack of Point and Penpol Smelting Works. This was taken down in 1910.

The same scene almost a hundred years later - April 2002.

The trees have grown as have the houses on Restronguet Point. There are more boats on Carnon Mine beach and, unlike the previous picture, we know the identity of the person in the foreground - Marie Bird.

Taking the Shopping Home.

The Old Tram Road was still a rough track when this picture was taken, during the last war. There was no vehicular access to Carnon Mine. You bought your groceries in the village and got them home the best way you could. This shows Mary Carlyon (always known affectionately as Aunt Mary in Carnon Mine) pushing her wheelbarrow full of shopping home from Devoran. Her dog was named Hitler.

Mary Carlyon - Carnon Mine.

Aunt Mary has arrived home with her shopping.

Old Carnon Miners.
Ralph Bird's maternal great grandparents - Fred and Julia Amelia Bryant. Fred was born in 1855 and died in 1939, Julia was born in 1851 and died in 1929. They had eleven children of which my grandfather was the tenth. They moved from Point to Carnon Mine in 1890. What furniture and possessions they had were taken to Carnon Mine by boat.

Launch of the 'Ophelia' at Carnon Mine.
Fred Bryant built the 'Ophelia' for his cousin Eddie Dunstan of Devoran. The year is 1929. The men in the picture are (left to right): Percy Trenoweth; (boy with the camera) Victor Moxam; behind him Will Trebilcock; Albert Tregunna; Edward Bryant; Fred Bryant; Charlie Trebilcock.

Carnon Mine 1929.
This was the year my great grandmother died. The picture was taken some time after the funeral. My great grandfather is seated on the left. The 'Hedge' was a popular meeting place for the men to meet on Sundays and swap yarns.

Eddie Hitchens and his Fish Barrow
at Carnon Mine 1940s.
Eddie was a local fisherman who often rowed or sailed as far as the Manacles to catch fish. He would then sell his fish between Point and Devoran. Eddie was a brother to Tom Hitchens, a well known boat builder who lived at Carnon Yard.

Royal Sturgeon September 1921.

This is a rare picture of a Royal Sturgeon, caught at Restronguet Weir. Early in the morning, Ralph Bird's great grandfather, Fred Bryant, and one of his sons, Dick Bryant, shot their seine net at Weir. They felt something go in the net, but thought it was a log of wood. On pulling the net in, they discovered this fish, but did not know what it was. It lay on the beach at Carnon Mine all day, until a gentleman from the village identified it. It was taken to Falmouth in Eddie Hitchens' boat, where they received £5 for it. In the photograph, left to right, are Marjorie Bryant, Charlie Bryant, Vinnie Jones and Norman Palmer. The picture was taken by Fred Pellow.

My Great Grandfather, Fred Bryant, with one of the Family's Dredging Boats.

They had three: 'Johnny Blight'; 'Hilda'; and the 'Polly'. The latter two were built by Charlie Ferris of Pill Creek. He was a brother to William 'Foreman' Ferris, builder of the 'Rhoda Mary'. In the stern of this boat - the 'Johnny Blight' - can be seen the seine net.

***Dick Bryant Cleaning a Seine Net
on Carnon Mine Beach.***
With him is his daughter, Marjorie Bryant, who later
married Arthur Tregaskis.

'Daisy Belle'.
The 'Daisy Belle' was built in 1895 by William Braybyn at Calenick for the cost of £6. She was built for Joe Nicholls, a Devoran man, who also owned the barge 'Maggie'. 'Daisy Belle' proved to be a very successful boat, winning many races at local regattas. She is pictured here under sail, with her original rig, off Flushing. She is now owned by the National Maritime Museum, Cornwall, where she has undergone a complete restoration - 2007.

Dick Bryant, Mending Nets at Carnon Mine.
He made his own nets and according to local knowledge was exceptionally fast at doing it.

CARNMARRIN, DEVORAN RIVER. 8.

Carnon Mine c. 1923.
A scene where there has been little change and, except for the fact that four feet was taken off the top of the mine building in 1983, the photograph could have been taken recently. The two men in the boat are Charlie Trebilcock and Fred Bryant. The head of Fred's dog, Tinker, can just be seen looking over the bow of the boat, which is called 'Bronco'. Fred built her in 1912. The picture is certainly after 1921, as the boat with the white inside alongside the mine building was built in 1921 for Will Trebilcock who can be seen in front of the mine building. She was named 'Kitty' after Will's sister.

The 'Erimus' off Carnon Mine.

The 'Erimus' has stopped off Carnon Mine to wait for the tide. Nowadays it would be impossible for a ship of this size to get up to Devoran because of the silting.

'Pride of the Hills' 1929.

The 'Pride of the Hills' was built for Cap'n Charlie Trebilcock. Two of his sons, Dick and Charlie, are seen here having rowed from Devoran to Porthoustock (approximately 11 miles) to watch the regatta. The boy standing in the stern is not known.

Bleak House c. 1926.

At this time, Bleak House at Carnon Mine was occupied by the Trebilcock family. They formed the band purely to raise money for charity. Members varied depending on who was available on the day. Shown here are, left to right: (back row) 'Farmer' Trebilcock (no relation to the Bleak House Trebilcocks); Will Trebilcock; Gordon Marshall; Reg Mitchell; — Marshall; (front row) — Trebilcock; — Trebilcock; — Trebilcock; Charlie Trebilcock.

Bleak House Band again, but a Slightly Different Line-up.

Left to right: (back row) 'Farmer' Trebilcock; — —; Will Trebilcock; —Trebilcock; Reg Mitchell; (front row) Charlie Trebilcock; — —; — Trebilcock; — Trebilcock.

Devoran Regatta 1947.
This is off Carnon Mine and shows the men's 'Pair of Paddles' race. A well known Falmouth rower, John Lowry, is in the lead in his boat 'Red Star'.

Carnon Mine c. 1955.
Little has changed except the two cottages on the right are now one. The young man sitting on the boat is Ron Hammett.

The 'Shamrock'.

This, and the following photo, were taken c. 1961, when the barge 'Shamrock' was in the Devoran River carrying out test drilling for alluvial tin samples. It is near to Christmas time as there is a Christmas tree at the top of her mast - an old sailors' tradition.

The 'Shamrock'.

The 'Shamrock' drilling for tin samples in the Carnon River.

The Barge 'Shamrock' near Carnon Mine c. 1961.

This picture was taken in 1961 when the 'Shamrock' was being used for exploratory bore hole drilling for alluvial tin deposits in the Carnon River. She is now preserved at Cotehele Quay on the river Tamar.

Gordon Marshall Collecting Fire Wood from Carclew Woods.

Gordon is seen here unloading fire wood at Well's Beach. The boat is the 'Eighty-One'. This was the last boat built by Tom Hitchens at Carnon Yard. Tom was eighty-one years old when he built her, which is how she got the name.

Relaunching 'Endeavour' 24th April 1982.

'Endeavour' was built as a lugger in 1910 by Trevorrows of St. Ives. She was built for the Humphreys family of Mousehole. Shortly after she was sold to the Merryfield Brothers of Pill Creek. In 1981 she was sold to Joe Keats and Robin Taylor. She was towed to Carnon Mine and given a major refit during the winter of 1981-82. This is relaunch day - pictured here are Joe Carlyon and Gordon Marshall.

Carnon Mine Beach.

This was taken on 24th April 1982, the day we relaunched the 'Endeavour'. These are some of the people who helped. They are, left to right: Reg Mitchell, Jim Sedgemoor, Peter George, Gerald Hodge, Bill Marshall, seated is Arthur George.

Carnon Mine Beach.

The three men are local - left to right they are: Peter George; Arthur George; and Jim Sedgemoor. Taken on 24th April 1982. The boat is the 'Jo Jo' built by William Brabyn at Calenick c. 1905.

'Bryanek' Gig being Built.

This is the gig Ralph Bird built for St. Agnes on the North coast of Cornwall. The picture was taken the day she left the workshop. Altogether Ralph Bird has built twenty-nine gigs here, plus four small rowing boats. His great uncle, Fred Bryant, built about twenty rowing boats on the same site making a total of fifty-three boats built in Carnon Mine. This is besides all the boats that were repaired as well.

Snow at Carnon Mine 1985.

It seems to be a rare sight in Cornwall now, but there was snow three years running at this time 1984, 1985 and 1986. The vessel on the beach is the 'Hope' built at Porthleven in 1907. The boat in the foreground with the cover is the working boat 'Endeavour' built as a lugger at St. Ives in 1910 for Mousehole owners.

Carnon Mine Engine House July 2000.

This is one of the oldest engine houses in Cornwall, although little remains of the building. It closed in 1843. In 2000, the Parish Council and English Heritage funded the restoration of the building.

Point and Penpol Regatta 2000.
The working boat 'Leila' just before the start of her race. Carnon Mine in the background.

Devoran Pilot Gig.
Pilot gigs are now a normal sight around Cornwall, but it is not often they are seen sailing. This is the 'Fear Not', Devoran's first gig, off Carnon Mine 2005. The mainsail is a dipping lug.

Very high tide at Carnon Mine.

This is me (author, Ralph Bird) sat on the seat above the beach, the date is 27th October 2004. The senior citizen at Carnon Mine (Bill Marshall) could not remember a higher tide in his lifetime. At the 'Pandora Inn', Restronguet, the water was up to the bottom of the window ledges.

'Buller' during her Restoration in 2006.

'Buller' was the first gig I built. Built for Cadgwith near the Lizard. She was named after a local man, Buller Arthur. She was the first of twenty-nine gigs built in Carnon Mine.

Chycoose Beach.

This is Chycoose Beach, near Point - or to give it its correct name Chypit. The black shed was at one time a sail loft. It has long since disappeared. This picture was taken in 1931.

Chycoose Beach or Chypit.

The rowing boat still has her culch boards in aft, although it is not the dredging season. Owners would sometimes leave the boards in place to enable them to carry a seine net. Note the absence of houses on Restronguet Point.

Chycoose c. 1920.

Point beach and Chypit

Point Beach 1911.

This beach is topside of the bungalow named 'Gulls Haven'. The beach was used by local river men to scrub and paint their boats, until it was shut off to the public. The name of the working boat is not known.

Penpol Wesleyan Sunday School Marching up to Point Green 1911.

Penpol Wesleyan Tea Treat c. 1919.

Penpol Smelting Works c. 1905.

This is a group of men employed at the smelting works. Fourth from the right, holding the large shovel, is Ralph Bird's great grandfather, Frederick Bryant; fifth from the left is his brother, John Bryant.

Creek Cottage c. 1925.

This is the cottage Ralph Bird's family - Bryants - lived before moving to Carnon Mine in 1890.

Point.

Point looks a very isolated spot in this picture compared to what it is like today. The picture is before 1910, as the stack was taken down that year.

The Beach on Western Side of Point Quay c. 1950.

Many of the rivermen or oyster fishermen kept their boats here, but it was shut off when the house alongside the beach was renamed 'Private'! Devoran is in the far distance.

THE RIVER FROM POINT LOOKING TOWARDS DEVORAN. 13.

The Beach by 'Gull's Haven' at Point.

This beach was used by rivermen and oystermen to moor their boats. It appears to be fitting out time as the boats are freshly painted.

Off Point Quay.

A well known photograph that has been used many times, but still captures the atmosphere of what Point used to be like. It is pre-1910.

Point from Carnon Yard c. 1909.

On the right is Penpol smelting works, which closed in 1921. On the left is Point lead smelting works. The stack on the left was taken down in 1910.

Penpol Smelting Works c. 1915.

This must have been after 1910, as the stack of Point lead smelting works has gone. This would have been above the clump of trees on the left of the picture. Penpol smelting works closed in 1921, but in this picture it is still going strong.

Point and Penpol 1950.

Almost the same scene, but about forty years later. There is no sign of either smelting works, but housing development has started.

The Old Water Mill just up from the Head of Penpol Creek.

It was later demolished for house building.

The Old Bridge at the Head of Penpol Creek.

The motor boat in the foreground is the 'Sunbeam' built by Pascoe's at St. Just in Roseland. Her last owner was Joe Carlyon of Carnon Mine around 1955.

At the Head of Penpol Creek.

Point c. 1946.

The gentleman pushing the barrow - is he responsible for the beautifully kept garden on the left? The garden is now an orchard and is maintained by the Point Quay Association.

Point Green as it used to look c. 1910.

It would be nice to know who the children were.

Point and Penpol Regatta c. 1946.

This was taken before the racing had started as the working boats have not hoisted their staysails. The 'Shamrock' is being used as the committee boat. The working boat to the left of 'Shamrock' is the 'Harriet'.

Point and Penpol Regatta.

The year is not known. There is very little wind and so the working boats are carrying topsails. As in the previous picture the race has not started as there are no staysails up.

Two well known local characters – Reg Mitchell and Reg Crocker.

Point and Penpol Regatta c. 1935.

This is not an actual view of the regatta, but shows boats and people gathering for the start. Note the coach and car on the quay.

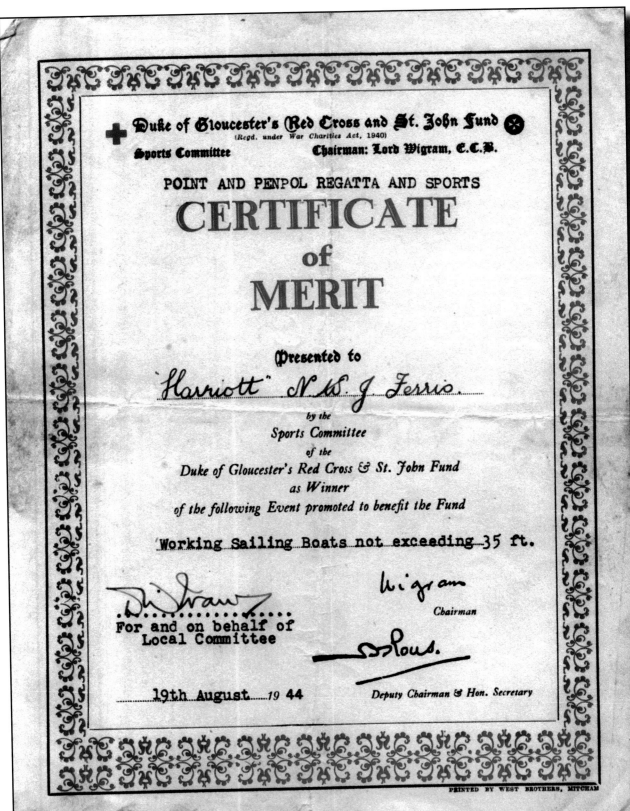

Duke of Gloucester's Red Cross and St. John Fund
(Regd. under War Charities Act, 1940)
Sports Committee   Chairman: Lord Wigram, G.C.B.

POINT AND PENPOL REGATTA AND SPORTS

CERTIFICATE
of
MERIT

Presented to

"Harriott" N & J Ferris

by the
Sports Committee
of the
Duke of Gloucester's Red Cross & St. John Fund
as Winner
of the following Event promoted to benefit the Fund

Working Sailing Boats not exceeding 35 ft.

Wigram
Chairman

For and on behalf of
Local Committee

19th August 19 44

Deputy Chairman & Hon. Secretary

PRINTED BY WEST BROTHERS, MITCHAM

94

Point and Penpol Regatta 1925.
This is Charlie Trebilcock winning the men's 'Pair of Paddles' race in the 'Kitty'.

Point and Penpol Regatta c. 1925.
It has to be after 1924, as the boat is the 'Maid Nancy' built by Tom Hitchens locally at Carnon Yard in 1924. She was built for Conybeare Bryant, of Mylor.

Point and Penpol Regatta c. 1950.

Point and Penpol Regatta was, and still is, one of the most popular regattas on the sailing circuit. At its beginnings, it was known as Devoran, Perranwharf and Point Regatta. This picture was taken in the early 1950s. There is a Falmouth sunbeam with just its mainsail up. In the top right hand corner are poles used for sheaf pitching - all part of the regatta sports.

Point and Penpol Regatta c. 1948.

There is a general variety of rigs here, but the most unusual are the Troy Class on the left - no. 14 (called 'Turquoise') and no. 9 ('Maid of Foye'). These two boats were owned in Flushing for a short period. They are a class usually associated with Fowey, where they still race on a regular basis.

Point and Penpol Regatta c. 1950.

Here we see the Falmouth working boats, or, to give them their correct name, the Truro River oyster boats. The boat on the right looks like Jimmy Morrison's 'Mayflower'. She has crosstrees on her mast, at that time, the only working boat to carry them. 'Mayflower' was built in 1905 by Richard Kitto, of Porthleven, for St. Ives owners.

Point and Penpol Regatta 2006.

The 28 ft working boat 'Grace' in the foreground wins the big class of the working boats. The little sailing dinghies are having a good race in the background. The local regatta is enjoyed by all sizes.

Point & Penpol Regatta.

The colourful spectacular Falmouth working boats are still a special and wonderful sight at the Point and Penpol Regattas today as they were in yesteryear.

Monday Night's Point & Penpol Rowing Regatta – Locals Watching the Gig Racing.

Point Regatta June 2003.

At this local regatta the sailing is held on a Saturday, followed by the rowing on the Monday evening. For three consecutive years (2002-04), the Falmouth lifeboat paid a visit. The lifeboat is a Severn Class with Caterpillar engines developing 2,500 hp, giving a top speed of 26 knots.

Due to the tide, the lifeboat has a limited time at Point Quay.

Here she is leaving, along with the Falmouth inshore lifeboat. The cost of a Severn Class lifeboat is around two and a quarter million pounds.

The Tram Road.

The Tram Road was officially made into a road in the early 1950s and so this picture was taken before that date, as there are huge puddles on the track, but it is after 1925 as Reg Crocker's bungalow, on the left, was built then.

Penpol.

The three children posing for this picture at Penpol are (from left to right): Bridget Collins; Graham Crocker; and Jean Lapham (neé Trebilcock). The picture was taken in Penpol at 'Stomps' (where the boatyard is now).

Looking into the Head of Penpol Creek c. 1950.
This shows the remains of the old sluice gate - now known as the Stepping Stones.

Point Quay and House c. 1955.
Jimmy Ferris, known locally as Jimmy Nor, later built rowing boats here in the workshop on the right.

An Early Aerial Picture of Point.

This was taken in the late 1940s, before any housing development in the area. Note the cultivated fields along Rope Walk, also the number of rowing boats in the bottom right hand corner on Point Beach.

Penpol Boatyard , the view from Trolver c. 1980.

The boat in the centre with the large wheelhouse is the old St. Ives fishing gig 'Cape Cornwall'. The large fishing boat with the two masts is the former fishing boat 'Hope', built at Porthleven in 1907 by Richard Kitto. The old Motor Torpedo Boat shown in the picture as a landing stage, was bought for £30 by the Hicks Brothers when they started Penpol Boatyard in 1948. It was broken up in the late 1980s.

'Mary' of Truro.
This shows the 'Mary' of Truro on Yard beach in 1927. Local boatbuilder Tom Hitchens is probably doing some caulking or some type of repair watched over by Cap'n Charlie Trebilcock.

Locally built Schooner the 'Rhoda Mary'.

Of all the vessels built at Carnon Yard, probably the most famous was the schooner 'Rhoda Mary'. Built with two masts, she was later converted to three. The yard at this time was owned by John Stephens of Devoran, but the actual building and designing of the vessels was carried out by William Ferris, along with other shipwrights. The 'Rhoda Mary' is seen in this picture sailing up the Mersey on 23rd June 1923. After the war she was abandoned on the river Medway.

Carnon Yard, December 1981.

This is a job Ralph Bird did on Yard beach - fitting a new false keel to the 'Hope', built in Porthleven in 1907 by Richard Kitto. It was a tricky job as the boat had to be pulled over on her side with a Land Rover and block and tackle. Pictured here are Chris and Charlie Warren.

View from the Top of Restronguet Hill c. 1950.

The 'Pandora Inn' is just out of the picture on the right. Point Quay and Penpol Creek are clear to see. The mast showing, just right of centre, belongs to the Thames barge the 'Heron'.

Restronguet Point c. 1950.

A view looking across showing the whole of Restronguet Point before any housing development had begun. The moorings in the creek, like the housing, started to spread about the same time.

'Mary' barge off Marblehead, Restronguet c. 1925.

Picking up oysters just above the 'Pandora' c. 1955.
Oyster fishermen would sometimes lay their catch on beds until a later date, when they would fetch a better price. The men in the picture are three Trebilcock brothers: Charlie, Will and Ted.

View from Ferry Point 1950.

Today, this area is full of yachts and other craft - something that escalated from the 1960s, but when this was taken, there appears to be only one mooring.

View from Ferry Point in the early 1950s.

The 'Pandora' is just out of the picture to the left. The name of the rather splendid motor yacht is not known.

Restronguet Point c. 1900.

This is taken from the 'Pandora Inn' looking across to Restronguet Point (pronounced 'Restrongit' or by locals as 'Strongwich'). The point itself is even today known as Ferry Point, originally from the time when there was a passenger ferry from point to the 'Pandora'. There is a barge on the left and a man sailing a boat with a lug sail.

Restronguet.

Little has changed in this photograph at Restronguet. There are boats in the dock and at this time many of the Ferris family lived in the cottages behind the dock. They are, left to right: Riverside Cottage; Rose Cottage; and Mellow Cottage. The 'Pandora Inn' can be seen on the left.

Looking from Restronguet Point across to Restronguet Weir.

Ferry Point at Restronguet.

This is Ferry Point with the Ferry Bell, which originally came from the steamer 'Penpol', one of the Chellew Fleet, seen here still in place. It was used to summon the ferryman from the 'Pandora' side of the river. The bell mysteriously disappeared just after the war.

Tensy Ferris.
This local character is Tensive Ferris or Tensy as he was known. He was one of William Ferris' sons. Tensy was at one time landlord of the 'Pandora Inn', which is behind his left shoulder on the other side of the river. Part of the landlord's contract was to operate the foot ferry between the 'Pandora' and Ferry Point. It looks as if Tensy has rowed across for water, as he has two pitchers with him.

Picking Flowers at Restronguet
c. 1935.
On the left is Monica Ferris - later Truscott - the lady in the centre is Granny Ferris, wife of Tensy and on the right is another Ferris.

The 'Pandora Inn' c. 1910.

This was in the days when it was still a riverman's pub. On the left is Billy Harris, who owned the 'Morning Star'. In the middle is Charlie 'Shanky' Ferris, Brian Ferris' grandfather and on the right is my great grandfather, Fred Bryant. His nickname was Gi - short for giant.

The 'Pandora Inn' 1924.

At this time the landlord was Tensy Ferris, grandfather to Andrew Ferris and Bill Marshall. Running the ferry to Restronguet Point was also part of the landlord's job.

111

The 'Pandora Inn' c. 1947.

At this time it was still a local mainly for rivermen. Then it still had a six day licence - it closed on Sundays. Now one of the river's favourite watering holes.

The 'Pandora Inn', c. 2000.

Taken early one Sunday morning, which is why the pontoon is looking so unusually empty.

Restronguet c. 1955, before the River filled up with Moorings and Boats.

The lug and mizzen boat is probably on the way up to take part in Point and Penpol Regatta as are the people in the other boat.

The Gut.

This stretch of water at Restronguet is known locally as the Gut. It is where the river reaches its narrowest point. There is quite a tide run here on spring tides. The working boat stern on just right of centre is the 'Florence', the black one is the 'Maid Nellie'.

Restronguet Point c. 1900.

Although not a clear picture, it is nonetheless a rare one. There are only five cottages on Restronguet Point - a far cry from today's number. There is an inside barge tacking down the river and bottom left can be seen a steam coaster discharging her cargo into lighters.

Restronguet Point before Modern Development c. 1930.

The first of the new houses has been built, as can be seen on the left of this picture.

Aerial view Restronguet Point.

Another early aerial view this time of Restronguet Point. It is probably about 1950. There is little or no building development taking place, Note also the lack of boat moorings. Although it looks as if the land is covered in snow it is just an over-exposed photograph.

Looking across to Ferry Point c. 1935.

The only houses are the two built by one of the Ferris family back in the 1800s.

Shipping in the Port of Devoran on night of 1861 Census. (Sunday April 7th).

Name of Vessel	Port of Origin	Tonnage	Description
Mary	St. Ives	67	Schooner Coasting
Brothers	St. Agnes	70	Schooner Coal Trade
Elizabeth	Truro	65	Coasting
Olive Branch	Gerrans Port Falmouth	62	Schooner Coasting
Isabella	Truro	135	Schooner Coasting Trade
Selina	Falmouth	82	Schooner Coasting Trade
Tigris	Falmouth	79	Schooner Coasting Trade
Azores Packet	Falmouth	63	Schooner Coasting Trade
Heligan	Truro	94	Schooner Coasting Trade
Susan	Plymouth	122	Schooner Coasting Trade
Union	Falmouth	81	Schooner Coasting Trade
Dove	Falmouth	71	Schooner Coasting Trade
Thomas Rising	Yarmouth	95	Brigantine (?)Home Trade
Mincwilo	Truro	90	Schooner
Matilda Elizabeth	Falmouth	114	Brigantine Coasting
John Wesley	Penzance	75	Schooner Coasting
Mary Simmonds	Truro	110	Schooner Coasting
Gipsy Queen	Plymouth	756	Barque Canadian
James	Llanelli	73	Schooner Coasting
Cornish Diamond	Truro	99	Schooner Coasting
Exchange	St. Ives	74	Brigantine Coasting
William & Ann	Plymouth	44	?Smack Coasting
Edward	Truro	53	Sloop Coasting
Brilliant	Truro	206	Ship Coasting
Merton	Truro	127	Schooner Coasting
J.S.T.	Truro	127	Schooner Coasting
Devonia	Padstow	70	Schooner Coasting
Apollo	Norway	—	—